Recycling, Yes or No

Erin Palmer

rourkeeducationalmedia.com

Scan for Related Titles
and Teacher Resources

Teaching Focus:

Endings- ed –ing- Locate the words recycled and recycling in the book. Write the words and underline the common root word. Then compare the endings. How does each ending change the meaning of the root word? Practice using the endings with another root word.

Before Reading:

Building Academic Vocabulary and Background Knowledge

Before reading a book, it is important to set the stage for your child or students by using pre-reading strategies. This will help them develop their vocabulary, increase their reading comprehension, and make connections across the curriculum.

1. *Read the title and look at the cover. Let's make predictions about what this book will be about.*
2. *Take a picture walk by talking about the pictures/photographs in the book. Implant the vocabulary as you take the picture walk. Be sure to talk about the text features such as headings, Table of Contents, glossary, bolded words, captions, charts/diagrams, or Index.*
3. *Have students read the first page of text with you then have students read the remaining text.*
4. *Strategy Talk – use to assist students while reading.*
   - *Get your mouth ready*
   - *Look at the picture*
   - *Think…does it make sense*
   - *Think…does it look right*
   - *Think…does it sound right*
   - *Chunk it – by looking for a part you know*
5. *Read it again.*
6. *After reading the book complete the activities below.*

Content Area Vocabulary
Use glossary words in a sentence.
environment
fumes
landfills
recycle
recycling plants
waste

After Reading:

Comprehension and Extension Activity

After reading the book, work on the following questions with your child or students in order to check their level of reading comprehension and content mastery.

1. *Why is it important to save our natural resources? (Infer)*
2. *What does the recycling symbol mean? (Summarize)*
3. *What is another way you can care for the environment? (Text to self connection)*
4. *Why is it important to remove all chemicals from things being recycled? (Infer)*

Extension Activity

Landfills and recycling offer different options for trash. Each affects the environment differently. With the help of an adult, gather up some garbage such as a banana peel, piece of newspaper, an eggshell, and a piece of a plastic cup. What would happen to each item if left in a landfill? Bury the items in separate holes in the dirt outside. Create little garden tags identifying what object is buried. After 4 weeks dig up each item. What happened? Which items changed and which did not? How does recycling help the environment?

Table of Contents

Introduction

Recycling is an important part of taking care of the **environment**. Though recycling can help the planet, is it always the best choice? Before you decide when to **recycle**, here are some things to think about.

Arguments for Recycling

Garbage is not good for the planet, but people create a lot of it. Think of the things you throw away every day, such as juice boxes and paper.

All of that trash gets sent to **landfills**, where it sits in a huge pile and may pollute the environment.

There are about seven types of plastic we use every day, but only two of them are recyclable.

Recycling is something that people can do to make the giant pile of garbage a bit smaller. Instead of throwing things away, recycling makes new things out of old materials.

Made from 100% recycled material

When the new things have been used up, they can often be recycled all over, creating a cycle of old to new and back again. That's why the recycling symbol is made up of three arrows creating a loop.

The recycling process helps create less **waste** and saves important natural resources such as water, wood, and minerals.

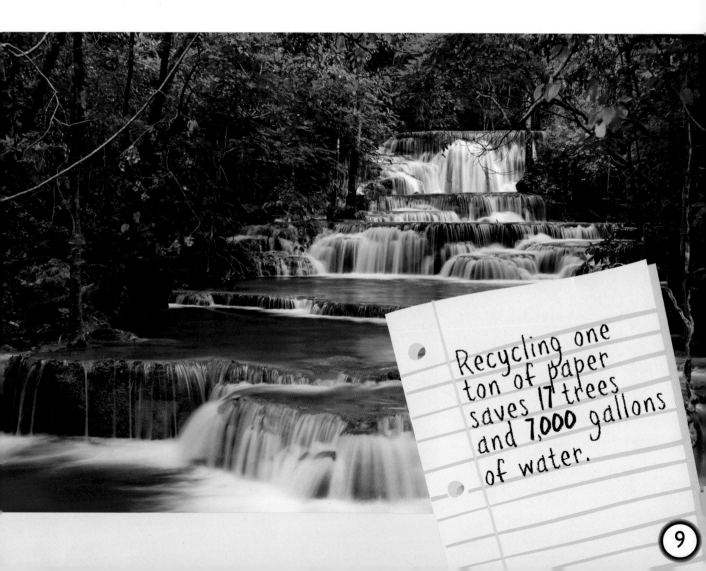

Recycling one ton of paper saves 17 trees and 7,000 gallons of water.

Arguments against Recycling

Even though recycling does a lot of good, there are times when it may not be the best choice to help the environment.

It costs about $4,000 to recycle a ton of plastic shopping bags. Reusable bags can be a better choice than recycling.

Protect the planet

Imagine an adult asks you to clean your room. You gather your toys, including some that were out in your muddy backyard.

When you bring the toys inside, your muddy shoes track dirt all over the house.

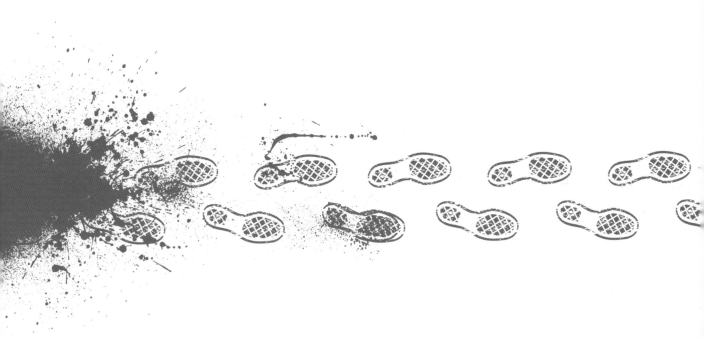

Does this room look clean? ▶▶

Though you put away your toys, you actually made your room messy in a different way by getting mud all over.

This is what sometimes happens with recycling.

Recycling may cause people to create more waste, because they don't think it will have any effect on the planet if they recycle.

If you drive a long way to recycle cans, the pollution caused by the car can hurt the environment, even though you are trying to help it by recycling.

Recycling plants can also create toxic **fumes** that are bad for the environment.

In some areas, recycling plants are considered the worst air polluters.

Recycling plants can pollute the air and deplete the ozone layer.

Some materials don't recycle well, because it can be hard to get the chemicals out of them during the recycling process.

The symbols on packaging tell you what can be recycled.

You Decide

How do you feel about recycling? Can you think of reasons why someone should or should not recycle? Write an opinion paper to explain your thoughts about this important issue.

Writing Tips

- Tell your opinion first. Use phrases such as:
  - *I like* _____.
  - *I think* _____.
  - _____ *is the best* _____.

- Give many reasons to support your opinion. Use facts instead of stating your feelings.

- Use the words *and, because,* and *also* to connect your opinion to your reasons.

- Explain your facts by using phrases, such as *for example,* or *such as*.

- Compare your opinion to a different opinion. Then point out reasons your opinion is better. You can use phrases such as:
  - *Some people think,* _____ *but I disagree because* _____.
  - _____ *is better than* _____ *because* _____.

- Give examples of the positive outcomes of someone agreeing with your opinion. For example, you can use the phrase: *If* _____ *then* _____.

- Include a short story about your own experiences with the topic. For example, if you are persuading someone that the best pet is a dog, you can talk about your pet dog.

- Restate your opinion so your reader remembers how you feel.

Glossary

environment (en-VYE-ruhn-muhnt): all of the surroundings and living things that make up the planet

fumes (fyooms): harmful smoke, gas, or vapor created by vehicles or machines

landfills (LAND-filz): land that is used to dump garbage or waste

recycle (ree-SYE-kuhl): taking an old product and using the material to make a new product

recycling plants (ree-SYE-kuhl-een plants): buildings where materials are recycled

waste (wayst): a material or product that has been used up

Index

Show What You Know

1. How can you tell if something is recyclable?
2. What are some things that cause pollution?
3. Why is recycling important?

Websites to Visit

www.pbskids.org/eekoworld/index.html

www.kids.niehs.nih.gov/explore/reduce

www.climatekids.nasa.gov/recycle-this

About the Author

Erin Palmer is a writer and editor in Tampa, Florida. She recycles every day. She has three dogs named Bacon, Maybe, and Lucky. Reading, traveling, and going to the beach are some of her favorite things.

Meet The Author!
www.meetREMauthors.com

www.rourkeeducationalmedia.com

PHOTO CREDITS: Cover (left): ©ranplett; cover (right): ©Rhea Magaro; page 1: ©Avava; page 4: ©robcruse; page 5: ©Alkindoza; page 6, page 18: ©Huguette Roe; page 7: ©Onur Donel; page 7 (right): ©bultozber; page 8: ©Wildpix; page 9: ©Noppakun Wiropart; page 10: ©Catherine Lane; page 11: ©Precip; page 12-13: ©Opka; page 14: ©Ralph125; page 15: ©David Parsons; page 16-17: ©JacobH; page 19: ©Evan Lorne; page 20 (left): ©AfricaImages; page 20 (right): ©Kate_Sept2004

Edited by: Keli Sipperley
Cover and Interior design by: Rhea Magaro

Library of Congress PCN Data

Recycling, Yes or No/Erin Palmer
(Seeing Both Sides)
ISBN (hard cover)(alk. paper) 978-1-63430-347-7
ISBN (soft cover) 978-1-63430-447-4
ISBN (e-Book) 978-1-63430-546-4
Library of Congress Control Number: 2015931675

Printed in the United States of America, North Mankato, Minnesota

Also Available as:
ROURKE'S e-Books